Curious George®
Haunted Halloween

Adaptation by C. A. Krones
Based on the TV special
Curious George: A Halloween Boo Fest
written by Joe Fallon

Houghton Mifflin Harcourt
Boston   New York

For information about permission to reproduce selections from this book, write to Permissions, Houghton Mifflin Harcourt Publishing Company, 215 Park Avenue South, New York, New York 10003.

ISBN: 978-0-544-32077-2 paper-over-board
ISBN: 978-0-544-32079-6 paperback

Design by Afsoon Razavi

www.hmhco.com

Printed in China
SCP 10 9 8 7 6 5 4 3 2
4500535491

AGES	GRADES	GUIDED READING LEVEL	READING RECOVERY LEVEL	LEXILE ® LE
5–7	1	J	17	480L

This year, George was spending
Halloween in the country.
The last autumn leaves were falling.
George and the man with the yellow
hat were busy raking.

Mrs. Renkins rode
by on her bicycle.
"Halloween's here! Hang on to your
hats!" she shouted.
"Happy Halloween, Mrs. Renkins!"
said the man.
George was curious. Why would he
need to hang on to his hat?

George went to the Renkinses' farm.
There were so many pumpkins!
His friends Allie and Bill were there, too.
"Hang on to your hats!" said Bill.

George and Allie were confused.
Why was everyone saying that?
"Haven't you heard of the Legend of
No Noggin?" Bill asked.
They hadn't.

Then Bill told them the spooky story:
A long time ago, there was a scarecrow
perched by Old Lonesome Tree.
It had a big pumpkin for a head, and a
hat on top.

But one Halloween, the pumpkin went missing.
From then on, everybody called the scarecrow No Noggin because it had no head.

No Noggin was angry.
What good was a hat without a head?
That's why every Halloween night, No Noggin shows up and kicks people's hats off!

George was spooked!
A headless scarecrow ghost?
"Don't worry," said Bill. "Just make
sure you hang on to your hat on
Halloween."

George went home with his pumpkin. He wanted to see his friend and find out more about No Noggin.

"It's just a legend, George," said the
man, "a tall tale, a ghost story—it's
not real."
But George wasn't so sure.

George and his friend decided to carve a
jack-o'-lantern.
George tried to get his mind off ghosts.
But he needed to know if No Noggin was
real.

The next night was Halloween.
George and Allie were hiding near
Old Lonesome Tree.
They were going to catch No Noggin
on camera.

Suddenly, they saw a shadow!
Could it be No Noggin?
George took a photo.

But it was only Bill in his wizard
costume.
Then George and Allie had an idea.
Bill could help catch No Noggin with
his wizard hat.

Bill stood near Old Lonesome Tree.
He walked back and forth and waited for
No Noggin to kick his hat.

Suddenly, Bill's hat flew off his head!
George and Allie chased the moving
hat into a cave.

Inside the cave, they found Bill's hat.
And Jumpy Squirrel.
And lots of other hats, all filled with
acorns!

There was no headless scarecrow!
It had been Jumpy all along.
Jumpy and his squirrel friends had taken
the hats to collect acorns.

George and his
friends had solved the mystery!
And they even had proof to show
everyone the truth behind the Legend
of No Noggin.

Well . . . maybe after Halloween.
Now it was time for George to put
on his costume and join his friends
for trick-or-treating.

Make Your Own Pumpkin Head

One of the best parts of Halloween is putting on a new costume. With these instructions, you can make a pumpkin mask that will fool anyone. Just be sure No Noggin isn't around to steal it!

What you need:
- a sheet of paper
- a paper plate
- scissors
- two pieces of string
- a hole punch
- a pencil
- markers, paints, or crayons
- tape or glue

Instructions:
1. On the piece of paper, use a pencil to trace your hand. Cut out your tracing and color it green. This will be your pumpkin stem!
2. Next, draw a face on the paper plate. It can be scary or silly, and it can have three eyes, a big mouth, or no nose! It's completely up to you!
3. Color your paper plate orange to look like a pumpkin.
4. Ask an adult to help you cut out two eyeholes and a mouth.
5. Tape or glue your stem to the top of the mask.
6. Punch one hole on each side of the mask, where the ears might be. Make sure there's enough room between the hole and the edge of the mask!
7. Tie a piece of string to each hole.

Now your mask is ready to wear! Ask someone to help you tie it on your head, and get ready to fool everyone with your very own pumpkin head.